TOMORROW

NEESHANT SRIVASTAVA

To the dreamers.

Contents

1. IT'S SO LONG

It's so long that men never tried,
That road uphill to the summit,
Where all endeavour subsides,
And we enter a new world blithe,
With warmth of heart and clear skies.
Where are those dark clouds,
Gathering above at the beck and call,
Of the longing soul loud,
For the darkest day that men recall,
To be free of the unending road.
It's so long and tiring,
For men to give up halfway,
And join all in frolicking,
To dampen the senses and disobey,
The very purpose of living.

2. THE DISTANCE

Many walked the mile,
Husband, father, employee,
Snuggling up to life free of exile,
Health, wealth, status and the story,
Easy fun shall be in style.
Why to be the hallmark of truth,
And bang one's head on the walls,
To live and suffer uncouth,
To walk to the cliff for the great fall,
And marry the dust and soot.
Very few know that there exists,
A road that leads to the land,
Of great beauty and rest,
First, they must believe in the wind,
And how we emerged from dust.

3. MY HERO

You left a life of ease,
And no one knows why,
To breathe in this horrid land,
A burning body and soul,
With not enough to wear,
For the sake of your children,
To give to them something precious,
That no gold could own,
Like the hammer on the stone,
To carve out a life out of nothing,
And then you left quietly,
With dreams of wonderland,
That did never come,
You have blessed me,
For I have found my way,
For a taste of life in all its glory,
And a chance to meet my real self,
Thank you.

4. BLOOM

It takes the earth for a flower to bloom,
It takes years for a tree of bark,
To suffer the tempest and noon,
And stand tall and unafraid of the dark,
All from a seed of boon.
People shall frolic and have fun,
Take a ship to a faraway shore,
Years in revel and glasses of rum,
Boxes of gold and cash to hoard,
An eternal life of fun to hum.
Suddenly they hear the clock ticking,
As if they missed the boat,
A deep hollow creeps in sickening,
After the frenzy loot,
For the gold and cash had no meaning.

5. PARDON ME

Pardon me for I have sinned,
To the man that kept me warm,
To the woman for stomach of brim,
To the house where I was born,
To the eyes that gave me dreams.
My sin of living in lust,
My anger like steam,
Even on people I trust,
My greed an endless scheme,
My pride a façade of husk.
I know not where I'll be,
After this life is over,
Maybe begging on bended knee,
For pardon to never,
To leave the sight of the anointed tree.

6. IT'S YOU NOT ME

Life is you, not me,
We are words and actions,
With a heart that longs to be free,
And touch others with compassion,
To lighten someone's days of grief.
It's a simple thing,
Yet no one seems to care,
Looking for their cut and swing,
Living in a shell aloof and unaware,
While to others suffering, they bring.
They do not know about the final day,
When all their ceremonies will end,
As they will be faced with questions nay,
Shoved into a dark dungeon,
Hare Ram Hare Ram is all they can say.

7. O! CHILD OF TODAY

Those old hats have perished,
Those words are heard no more,
Love on a busy street has vanished,
It is a very long road to that sacred door,
Are you lead astray O! puckish,
There are too many you say,
Keeping afloat is a hard task,
You may be lost in the hay,
And buy yourself a mask,
To cheat and get away.
It's not in someone to follow,
A road that is hard,
To consider failure as success and blow,
Like a free willing wind unheard,
O! Child of today, reach for the door.

8. THIS SUMMER

This summer lasted too long,
Humans baked like sand on a hot pan,
Clouds of smoke can do no wrong,
To feign the rain in vain,
The world does hide to hear a song.
Life has no escape for the earthly man,
His mind with collisions unending,
His peace is the graveyard sand,
Hot and cold none to his liking,
He waits for sunset and the band.
Lips of love and eyes of dove,
If only I could take you and run,
I have enough in my bag my love,
This woman, my wife, taciturn,
Take me O! woman of the grove.

9. LOVE A FEW

In a race for the upper hand,
When men bow low on passage,
When we are much in demand,
When money is the craze,
When darkness we feel where we stand.
When life is so easily sorted,
Without an inkling of something deep,
When our lives are uprooted,
With a simple wind in a reap,
By the devil in a whoop.
Little boy, why are you scared,
You don't know the game yet,
Perhaps you withstand and bare,
All in your heart you little pet,
They will kill you for sure.

10. A MAN HAS A WOMAN

I live my life through,
Jittery lows and easy highs,
I hoped to find my woman so true,
I waited on a sea of sighs,
For a woman so blue.
She did not come at dawn,
She was missing by night,
It would be a sin I am warned,
To hope for someone by twilight,
I'd rather pass unborn.
She did come after all I'm told,
A vision perhaps when it got too late,
Betrothed I was to a lovely lady of old,
As a young maiden to compensate,
For being single in my youth of gold.

11. THE EARTH NEVER HEARD

The earth never heard,
Millions is strife and pain,
The green blossoms towards,
A leafy jungle in sun and rain,
Flowers of glory unheard.
We shall stay for a while,
Before we go away somewhere,
Where the earth meets the skies,
For a little rest so dear,
While the earth whistles a lie.
That all is good in her laps,
A new morning is a new perspective,
Only to let the sadness stack,
Life of bliss hardly prospective,
Like a jocular bone we do lack.

12. PERHAPS

Perhaps I met you long ago,
And not live a loveless life,
If only I knew you too felt so,
When I was a lad of kites,
Too young for love of woes.
Why did I wait I don't know,
Like a fool for some destined day,
Looking into eyes as they go,
A promise until the dusk of grey,
To wait until the end and hope.
A dream you were I realized,
I loved you and I didn't know,
You were too tall among ladies dignified,
Graceful and the glow of snow,
I rub my eyes and hide.

13. THE WRATH

Don't play around for someone's wrath,
You can control but all,
On this mysterious life path,
Soon it may fall,
Like black rain of death.
A live lived then cannot be undone,
Deeds cannot be ironed,
It may be carefully hidden,
From a new world unlearned,
Don't look back good riddance.
Don't play around with fire,
Didn't your father tell you,
You are heavy with thoughts Sire,
Sleepless and nightmares new,
You can't run away or rewire.

14. HOW FAR

O! Mother I am a man of common soil,
How far will I go,
My land barren of sun and toil,
Every breath my last bow,
I died long ago in the foil.
I look for eyes that care,
I look for a heart deep,
And find none that wear,
A simple life truth in the leap,
To come closer to oneself in dare.
How far are the skies O! High,
Perhaps on a journey west,
I can reach emerald sky,
When the sun does rest in its vest,
And bid adieu to sinking eyes.

15. OVER SOON

Nothing lasts forever,
Soon we drift far away,
Into a world of newcomers,
That may not sway,
Enough to ruffle the sleeping monster.
For this is a world of ease,
With a ride on leather,
Ushered too early above the seas,
To a hill top with a feather,
On a cap sitting on the head unease.
Gone are those that try,
To unlock the mysterious,
Passage long and dry,
Easily lost by the industrious,
A shroud of darkness to walk by.

16. HEAR THEM FALL

Bit by bit I hear them fall,
My life if there was one,
Hope escapes my window sill,
Like waves in sand,
Did I ever long for a human touch,
The God Almighty in deep slumber,
Closing doors on me with thud of sin,
There perhaps lies some boat in the distance,
I cannot hear it wobble or thrash,
Or its hoot or holler,
This summer has been too long,
Like a forgotten flower,
I kiss the earthen breeze,
And dawdle aimlessly,
The dawn is about to break,
So I have heard a million times,
I have bequeath my youth to the Lord,
And as an old man I only pray,
Those youthful wishes have perished,
And so this body to dry and crumbling,
I prepare for an exit,
And wonder about the interim,
Am I my worst enemy.

17. LONG AGO

Long ago I heard the lovebird sing,
Just a touch and it flew way,
Lost in the distant skies,
Never to appear again,
I heard an aspiring soul,
Leading me into the dark dungeon,
Of death and nonexistence,
It gave no answers but directions,
Like a cruel master in total command,
Not a word to be uttered before the Master,
My life miles from the carnival,
My existence like a shapeless rock,
Thrown on the wayside to die,
I waited and did not move,
Until the spread of green fungi,
I opened my eyes to grey whiskers,
My love died a long time ago,
I still waited with baited breath,
Just in a moment I heard a screech,
Of a lofty bird that had flown too close,
It had probably flown for endless miles,
It was indeed the lovebird,
I suddenly rose from my grave,
To meet my lover of a lifetime,

TOMORROW

Perhaps of countless ages,
We were one together,
Never to part ever again,
While the world went globetrotting,
Fancy dresses and party of revels,
Changing lovers like the colour of the skies,
Just to find one true love.

18. DON'T GO TOO HIGH

Don't go too high,
Where the bushes can't hide you,
Far from the rattle of moths,
Or the hidden heat of swarming ants,
Or the prickly weed on wasteland,
Or the back current of waste,
With a smell that's nauseating,
Or the crumbling earth under your high rise,
The bleak cotton cloud hanging in the skies,
Or the mirky sun with a dull glow,
Or the waste you expel into the river,
The sky is picture blue for a take-off,
As you touch the heavens in your flight,
A house among the clouds you wish,
To give you an enchanting view,
But all shall end one day,
When you finally close your eyes,
As your body melts to the earth,
And your soul shall take a flight,
Like all ordinary souls.

19. WHY DIDN'T YOU

Someone asked why didn't you,
When the morning was high,
And you were young,
When birds succumbed so easily,
To a youthful body that sprung,
To catch a nook and eyes of rumour,
When carnal balloon squashed to rubber,
And freaky ties with a heavy crotch,
Was all in the game,
As the pages were flipped and flipped,
Where were you hiding my friend,
Why did you not dive in to the fun,
After all it lasts just a few moments,
And does not amount to anything,
What vows made you squander,
Your youth and your life,
Don't blame the other side of fifty,
This was the choice you made,
When those days are gone,
And will never come again,
Listen to the breeze of silence,
It shall come forth someday, perhaps,
And show you the way.

20. THE OTHER SIDE OF BEAUTY

I have seen beauty a plenty,
Sculpted bodies of snow,
Picture perfect with no blemish,
A dazzle to hold you forever,
Beautiful eyes, torso and plump,
Like a flower at its full bloom,
Too perfect for ordinary eyes,
They just float like angels,
Like the Gods at a tea party,
Gay abandon and sucking health drinks,
Or a glass of wine,
Nobody can hold their gaze for long,
They must pass swift,
Lest the queen stumbles on a frown,
On a perfect face,
A disgrace for the feminine corset,
The other side has strange noises,
Like someone whipped and slashed,
Wales and cries grow in number and intensity,
The crying grows louder and louder,
The beating carries on for an entire day,
Until it ceases for minutes,

There is blood all around,
Until the rampage is on again,
Is this the other side of beauty,
God forbid.